half
MYSTIC

is an internationally-acclaimed independent publishing house, literary journal, radio show, and arts organisation dedicated to the celebration of music in all of its forms. Half Mystic Press, our publishing arm, releases two to four books of prose, poetry, and experimental work per year—invocations of love, wildness, and uncertainty, the heartbeat of humanity set to a 4/4 time signature, expanding and redefining unsung narratives, sharp and lamenting, eyes on the horizon. For more information, books similar to this one, and submission guidelines, please visit www.halfmystic.com.

Praise for
Say Mother Say Hand

"Marie Conlan traces a lineage throughout *Say Mother Say Hand*, moving from allusions to the Seven Mothers of the World to the serpentine nuances of personal history. Through this debut she pioneers that lineage of examination, empathy, and experimentation-as-exploration. In Conlan's words, the traditions we turn and return to as we celebrate love and comfort ourselves through loss pupate and swell to be seen through a grippingly original lens. Here is a book of generations, of knuckles and lace, of treasures and 'remnants from an unknown sea.' Here are pages that are lovingly alive, filled with marrow."

—*David Welch*, author of *Everyone Who is Dead* and recipient of awards from the Academy of American Poets, the Poetry Society of America, and the Sewanee Writers' Conference

"Every family has a storyteller—one who takes note, digs deep, and attempts to make sense of the past. In this incredibly inventive and highly personal exploration of family, history, and trauma, Marie Conlan offers us ways to move beyond pain by taking the past and transforming it into 'something sweet to chew on, a salve, a story.' She reminds us that while we might not be able to escape our lineage, 'there's nothing to inherit,' and we have the power within us to make our own narratives, our own futures. Her incantatory language functions like a spell that moves to cast out the ways in which history tends to repeat itself. In the end, we are reminded that the cure for everything is always love."

— *Sara Veglahn*, author of *The Mayflies* and *The Ladies*

"In Conlan's memoir, we stand with her at the altar as she vows to her ancestors *not even death do us part*. Death and its close calls are what guide her (and us) through a hagiography of people who may or may not be worthy of being seen as heroes, heroines, friends, and shadows through the innocent, questioning eyes of a child, and the troubled, interrogative eyes of that child as an adult—eyes that are simultaneously passive receiver and active perceiver. Conlan writes, 'I begin to think if I have a little girl, I will name her after what you could have been,' inviting her family lineage to keep dreaming, repeating, stuttering, and 'looking for proof' of lives lived and yet to be lived. It is hard to know in this book who is sick and who is not, the sick and the healthy set against the backdrop of needy children, of needing children. What Conlan needs is to clear space within her body, one that is occupied by family, to make room for a lover who shows up like a lightning storm, causing steam to rise: 'if I could just fit his bones into my body.' At the same time, she needs to keep her family close because without them, she could not survive: 'make her stay in our bones.' Conlan catechizes these needs, breaks them apart, and puts them together again, satisfied or not, writing vibrant and brilliantly crafted scenes cut from memory, excised from her skin."

—*Karolina Zapal,* author of *Notes for Mid-Birth* and *Polalka*

FIRST PRINTING, APRIL 2020
HALF MYSTIC PRESS
www.halfmystic.com

EDITED *by* DANIE SHOKOOHI
DESIGNED *by* TOPAZ WINTERS

ISBN-13: 978-1-948552-10-3
ISBN-10: 1-948552-10-8

Say Mother

Say Hand:

An Anti-Memoir

Marie Conlan

A

Half Mystic Press

Publication

for three little girls

"'Are you watching?'

Everyone asked this question of everyone else in the family."

—Christine Schutt, *Florida*

Dear child,

Here are your bones. They are stuffed with the marrow of shaking blue cocoons. They will burst or you will grow them, but they will burgeon. They are breakable, cradle them. They are canvas. Rub their bruises into paintings, puddles, monuments, etc. Dear child, here are your bones. They are precious things.

All my love.

The caterpillars are growing in size.

You don't believe me no one believes me—

They are becoming the size of small dogs, crawling up her bedsheets and drinking from the catheter. She knows they are not real. They have induced a cold terror and deep paralysis. The doctors say her stabilized internal organs are no longer conducive to the ICU. I tell them caterpillars are not conducive to our kitchen. The caterpillars grow. She does not want to go   to the fucking psychiatry unit. I tell the nurses   my mother is not going to the fucking psychiatry unit. We move to an ambiguous recovery wing. The caterpillars dissipate into the phosphene of a calm sleep.

According to the science of genealogy, a lineage can be traced thousands of years back to the lives of just seven women. Quite literally, the mothers of the world. Some historians have reveled in writing imaginary tales of these women's lives, a fictionalized history constructed in desperate attempt to fill the void of a past lost in the patterns of mitochondrial DNA.

I call my mother and tell her we could find our mother. I could pay to send my DNA to a man dedicated to the analysis of human history, and in turn receive a typed declaration of our ancestry, a scientific declaration of our lineage. He can tell us who we are. She is excited. She says fantastic, she says   how wonderful. It costs $250, and she will pay for it.

The next afternoon, I speak with my mother again. I hear the hard ends of tulip stems fall sliced into the sink. She tells me about her day. The weather is dark, the dog is tireless, the husband is anxious. I don't remind her of the DNA testing, and she doesn't mention it again. There are only so many answers that make sense when you're paying a man to give them to you.

Sometimes, I imagine our mother is Haplogroup K, Mother Katrine. Polish, for "pure."

Before my father gets sick he says to the five of us
don't look for me when I die don't expect me to press my
ass on the end of a bed and flick the lights on and off. We
say   okay. When my father gets sick we feed him water
with a sponge. We say   look how strong he is look at
those gray hairs still clinging to his head. The week before
he dies my sister & I roll the garbage down the driveway
before school. He says   I am so proud of you. It is not
garbage day and we have to roll the bins back up the
driveway. I feel guilty like he is proud for nothing.

My sister says she has connected with our father. Her psychic felt our father's energy, saw him hold balloons in celebration of the first grandchild, said his presence was urgent and commanding.

I make an appointment with the psychic. I am hesitant, but I am selfish. I want more than twelve years and a few weeks of a mind on morphine. I want a conversation, I want a father, and I want God, and sixty dollars will do.

When I speak with the psychic, he says   who was the suicide. I say   my father died of cancer. He says no, the suicide. He says   your maternal grandmother is with you, anxious for communication.

He is insistent he feels her presence. I lose faith in his abilities. He tells me she is adamant I know her death was a suicide. I say   my father died of cancer. He says in the living room. I say   yes, in the living room. He says   your grandmother is with you.

Later, hesitantly, I tell my mother   the psychic says your mother killed herself. With brief, wet eyes, she says I know.

I remember my grandmother's death in small moments. I am four years old in the back of my father's white Infinity and he says   your mom's mom has died. I say why did she die. He says   old age.

My cousin cries into his palms at her funeral. I wonder what memories he is mourning. I hope for a burning sensation to bloom in my tear ducks. I stare at my heels hanging out the back of my glossy black shoes. A cold sweat sits in my feet, the seam line of my white tights has stretched beneath my toes. At the burial, I wander up the grass and look down at the people who are sad and huddled between stone pillars.

My father is cremated at the same cemetery a few years later. It is a Catholic cemetery; my father converted back to Christianity from Buddhism, weeks before he died. I recognize the stone pillars, filled with a blurry memory of people with sad faces, someone with a red coat. Sometimes, we visit my father and bring him plastic orchids. We do not visit my grandmother. Her grave is a flat headstone and often covered in snow.

My grandmother dies like this: naked in the hallway of her apartment building screaming   the nazis are comingthenazis are coming the nazis killing my mother my ff father fuckingget OFF megetoffme get off me youmother   flesh slapped palms all over doorways   fuckingmenASSHOLESgodDAMMIT & mistaking the police men for nazis restraining her keeping her alive having their way with her ridding of her done with her   the nazis arecomingFUCking arehearearefuckinghere why don't you just come FUCKME then   clothed in detox almost to the psych ward   officer let me grab my clothes so sorry officer so silly sorry silly so drunk my place my just down the street sir I'll be right back just my clothes please yes help I need help I I'll be right back thank you officer so sorry and   to the liquor store to the apartment to the couch quick fervent gulps fast now slumped now between couch and coffee table over now 42 proof waves of dark mind rape addiction work camp mind memories then gone and then god maybe.

On a weekend trip home from college, I sit in the kitchen with my mother, her fingers folded over the handle of a coffee cup. It is rare to catch her idle, not cleaning, moving, standing, asking what she can cook for me. I study her hands, knuckles like the aging skin of yellow peppers, folded into soft wrinkles. Her swollen bones ache from the arthritis burrowing in her thin wrists. Her fingers hold red jujubes, and she throws them between her cheeks, mouth smacking open and closed, her teeth chomping deliberately   these remind me of my daddy, he would always bring me candy. Her voice is childlike, blushing from her father's adoration.

I ask about her drinking because my step-father has been asking about her drinking.

She is fine she is fine she is fine

bullshit little trashed child all corner eyes always
dewy with booze always leaking breaking everything
waking me in the middle of the night   who is right
who is right he's so sick of your drunkface so sick of your
drunkmouth I tell him   he's right you're loaded
he doesn't have to break dressers about it there's livers dis
membered children all over the floor I tell him   stay
I tell you   goodnight   remember that mom
admit it admit bullshit this punch-drunk cucaracha
towing truck not funny not coming anymore he called and
said   the vodka is gone   I call and can't
understand you admit it

Her eyes move upward, reading script from the inside of
her forehead. She thanks me for awakening her, for loving
her, for saving her. She says   remind me I want you to
remind me. She says   I draw a box in my calendar on
the days I am sober honey draw me boxes I love you I'm
sorry. She says   honey draw me boxes.

When she drives me back to Chicago, we get to her hotel
room and shake off the eight hours of car ride. She opens a
bottle of wine, and we drink to our tiredness.

I play happy birthday on the xylophone, next to the static of a car radio. I play the xylophone on my lap, and three little girls crawl onto my knees. I do not know how to keep them there, so I offer them presents to unwrap from my fingers. I give the first little girl a Christmas cookie tin full of buttons. *For keeping?* she says. I nod. I tell her I have washed them, they are new things now. They are for her dolls, or to use as skipping stones. I give the second little girl a stuffed tiger. She looks bored. *You are a little girl* I say. She shakes her head no, but tucks the tiger loosely under her right arm. I give the third little girl a jumprope. *And what am I supposed to do with this!* she screams. *Jump rope,* I say, *in the grass.* Her throat blushes red little ponds all over it, she is having trouble timing her inhales with the immense exhale of her sobs. *You are a child!* I scream. *You are a child! You are a child! Jump rope! A child jumps rope!* She shakes her head violently and falls off my knee. I lose her, and cannot find her under the front seat carpet or the soles of my shoe. I throw the xylophone out the window. The other two girls disappear, leaving behind a trail of buttons and stuffing. I coil the jumprope in the cup holder, for next time.

ॐ

My mother texts   *love u!* to me and other people she
loves my mother tells my stepfather   leave leave
he doesn't leave just sleeps downstairs my mother says
justlikemymother   she crawls into bed she drinks
justlikemymother   more vodka she takes her benzos
whole palm fulls.

I text *love you mum!* I close my book at the end of my shift I shove my tips in the left corner of my bra I walk three blocks down Hennepin home.

The morning before, my mother types into her phone:

Had conversation about working (staging for realtors). Next morning having little to no memory of any details pertaining to that conversation. Even though mind is going 100 mph, I can't seem to put it together and it comes out slowly and distorted... Feeling great today. Feeling finally back to normal. Feeling "awake," like I was in a fog or somewhere else. Try to talk or act normal. Forced, like you know something is wrong. Overcompensated forced talk. As it relates to drinking seems like the thought process might be having a drink or two will get me to normal. No attention span.

Blue Morpho Butterfly Eats All the Amitriptyline and Flys

It leaves   a yellow dust   swimming in the toilet
bowl like water color   like piss   for all
the beauty we've ever found   in toilet bowls
flushing   similar to the sensation of swallowing
severed from hands   very small   tucked into a
wave   there is amitriptyline   in so much blood
whole palm fulls   palms with   such purpose
my mother is fine   hair wet like a mermaid's pulse
breath sour like winter plums   there is medication for
this   whole palm fulls   there is death for that
too   Mom   if you were craving that sensation
of a fleeting blue morpho butterfly   so badly that
escape into the night   when the moon is almost
all whole   the butterflies will not migrate   into the
kitchen first they are induced   caterpillars hanging
from the vine of the catheter   they almost reach you
the nurse finds you cowered   in the corner
booze pooling   caterpillars gorging   on your pores
we leave the caterpillars   to molt   the booze dries

17

the husband   divorced   the home sold
my father's love letters all over   the living room
fresh blue morpho butterfly   tattooed on your
shoulder   you remind yourself   you are fleeting
the moon is almost full stop reminding me   you   are
fleeting   there is medication for all of this
goodstuff benzos   whole palmfuls   I took
all of your medication   in a ziplock baggie
whole palmfuls   I am confusing the beauty
in the painting   with the piss in the toilet bowls
and the water   for a womb   the pills dissolved and
gone and   in another dream   the blue
morpho butterfly   eats all of the amitriptyline
and dies against the moon.

My stepfather calls while I am cross-legged on the wooden
floor of my apartment, while I am sorting socks, while I
am mid breath he says   there's been a   ah
everything is alright um   she was so drunk
talking about her mom said   leave leave   so I left
just downstairs I didn't leave her I left just downstairs I
didn't leave her   her vitals are okay
breathing and beating and warm flesh but fleeting
I didn't leave her the morning was the dog jumping on the
bed weird to see her idle not up moving asking what she
can make me and I tried   I   I tried to wake
her up she wouldn't wake up I tried to wake her up it had
been sixteen hours   maybe   I called
the ambulance she's not up she'sshe's in the ER we're
waiting and I left because theres no room to wait
I don't know   there's no room to wait we don't know
when she'll wake up   we'll go back   she'll wake up.

He takes me to get a burger and my sister comes and she
knows it is not okay and she knows we're supposed to be
at the hospital and I know we're supposed to be at the
hospital
          why aren't we there
          why aren't we there

He says   there is no room to wait   I'll wait
in the doctor's ass bring me to my mother. He brings me to
my mother he brings me to the ICU.

20

I call my lover I say   come   baby   please she's
dying she's here dying come   get here.

Once upon a time a mother. With fused legs. She gave birth through the throat stretched it wide open & a generation of prayer spattered like gunfire—three of them. Generations. And an origin she painted onto shells she used to cover her breasts to cork the milk from pouring into the sea, dissipating into small creamy circles.

There really was a girlhood. Look. House with driveway, TV, gel pens, named dolls, paint set, jump rope, three older sisters, one older brother, bike with radio, family dinner, & eventually, in desperation, a pool that changed colors in the dark.

Dear Mom,

Five 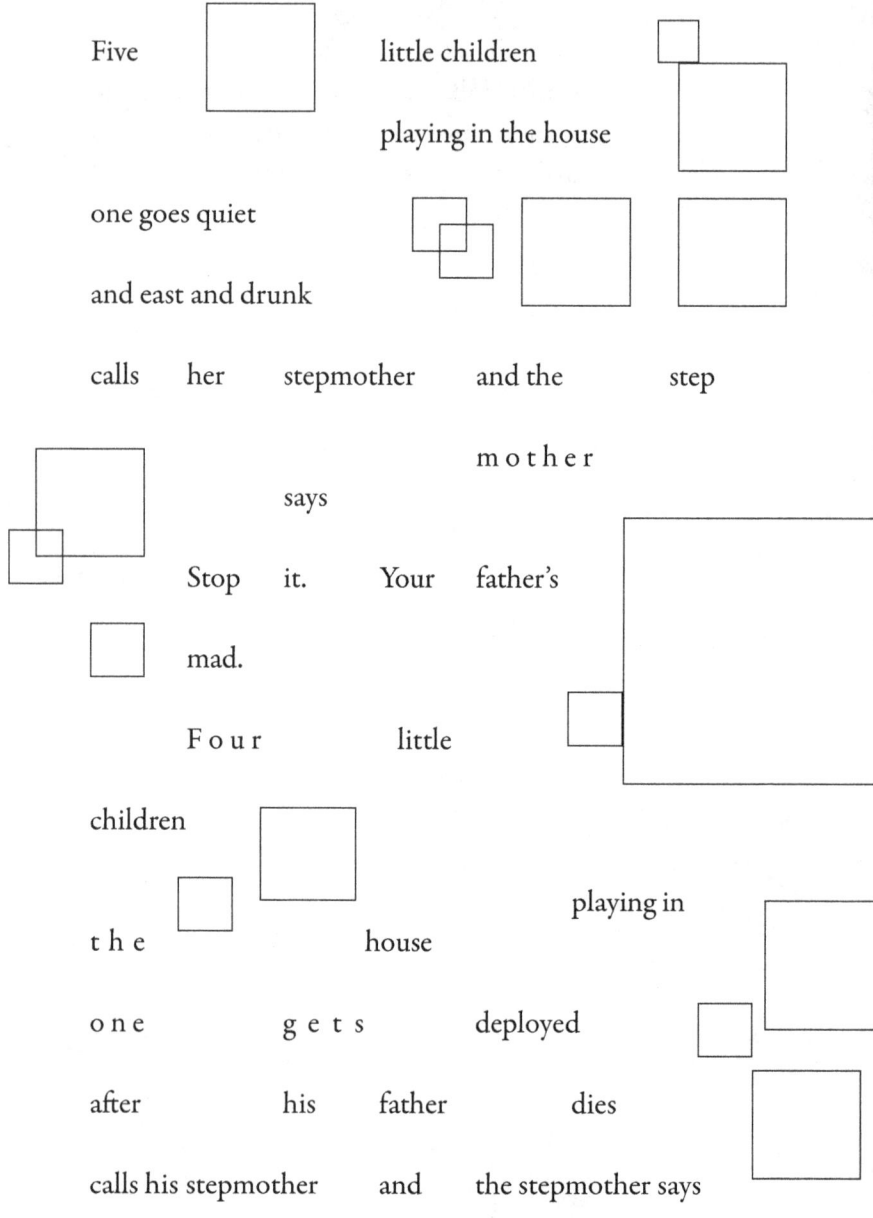 little children

playing in the house

one goes quiet

and east and drunk

calls her stepmother and the step

m o t h e r

says

Stop it. Your father's

mad.

F o u r little

children

playing in

t h e house

o n e g e t s deployed

after his father dies

calls his stepmother and the stepmother says

come back   for   a morphine   goodbye

from   a   hospice bed.

T h r e e   little children

playing in the house

one keeps the secrets

            for the dead and the drunk

       brings her stepmother to the doctor

and the doctor says   no more   benzos

in that sick little head.

T w o   l i t t l e   children

playing   in   the   house

o n e   makes a father

from paper   dolls taped   with   arms

says I'm   leavingI'm   leaving

25

One little child left

looking

says

mom

says mom

mom

My father dies when I am thirteen. Four years later, I fall in love. The sensation is almost unbearable, a crushing undulation that erodes parts of myself into the corners of my lover's body. I sleep tangled in him, between limbs and laced through fingers. I think of my mother, her body sturdy on the side of the hospice bed, curled tightly against the fragile bones of my father. I wonder what parts of her eroded into the nape of my father's neck, under the curved valleys of his knuckles, beneath the roots of the few hairs that held strong to his head. Parts of her I was still needing.

The psychic says I am an old soul. My therapist tells me I am the product of alcoholic parents and the product of a distant father. I am always fixing, pleasing, managing, care taking. In my college writing classes, I write about daddy issues. I make metaphors about arms. I think how this must be a profound insight into my destructive desire to fall into them, be carried by them, scooped up and salvaged. When I try to write about my relationships, every memory sounds like men crying in bedrooms, feels like the soft push of their cheek to my chest, tastes like the whispers I want down my throat   thank you for saving me.

I leave the hospital after hours of staring at my mother's eyes and wrists and cheeks, waiting for a voluntary flinch or a hollowing out of words, bracing every docile pulse and slow breath. Each noise from the live painting of her vital signs burrows in my central nervous system, a catalyst for guilty prayer breaths   IpromiseIpromise.

At night I leave her and my stepfather leaves her and she does not die alone that night but I will never forgive myself for leaving her. Will never understand all this leaving.

It costs me ten dollars a day to leave the hospital parking lot, ten dollars more than I have to pay for things like space. I would pay endless quarters or tickets or hours to never have to be reminded I am renting space to never have to be reminded that it cannot fill all of me. When I leave I grow anxious from movement, I can feel the whole world's spit and snore. An involuntary mechanism of an entire species. What about just one mother trying to inhale a room whole junkie caterpillars jonsing for all of her oxygen.

I leave her there. I leave with my lover we drive across the
river we get a quarter tank worth of gas I do not leave the
car I tell him   she can't die tonight she can't
shecan't shewon't die tonight she can't
IpromiseIpromise   into my lap and the sky and the
windshield   shecan'tshecan't and could die. And
cannot.

We park outside my apartment, we park in my designated space. I do not want to leave the car I kiss him so hard I climb into his lap can barely feel his collarbone or elbow or ribcage through his jacket and shirt and flesh I'm trying to get to the bones we do not make love I do not want to fuck I make my way down him I do not want to leave this space he is warm in my mouth my bones are suffocating my breath like how many ways could I fit him into me if I could just fit his bones into my body he could stretch my ribcage wide enough for more space to fit into he feels strange receiving me I am aching with a need to get my bones out of me swallow you make me into a space that could hold you any of these bones I am drowning in them I am trying to keep them in place I am trying I am she can't die tonight she can't she won't her bones she is still in her bones make her stay in our bones make her stay make her IpromiseIpromise.

& In the morning she wakes up and I ask if that means she
will make it and the nurse says   I don't know.
And I ask the doctor what this means and he says
I don't know. She wakes up again and I ask her what now
and she says   I don't know.

A mermaid saves a city. Names a city. A mermaid with charred scales & hair fried lavender & jewels in her mouth as sucking stones as prayers a mouth stuffed with prayers couldn't even swallow them bursting from lips & falling like jelly. Slow congealed blood. Pressing treasures to her eyes, acorns. Can you imagine? The residue of the earth clinging to its womb like that. Could you imagine.

When my mother wakes up and she is talking and she is breathing and she is putting sentences together it is the best day of my life. She is tired from the detox and the hallucinations and the dying, but her face is bright and vivid. Warm. Ready to embrace at any moment.

Her lips are cracked and her voice is weak. I feed her water with a sponge. She looks childlike in the light of the hospital. Tired and so pure just a body in a bed and breathing. Tender eyes leaking. She hates it she apologizes
        I don't want to be my mother I am so sorry I do not want to be my mother here I am my mother.

She hates her crying and I do it for her. I let my cheeks grow salty, remnants from an unknown sea.

The caterpillars hatch at night. They begin to invade the seams of my mother's bed sheets and thin cotton gown. In a panic she pulls the gown over her head and throws it to the ground spiraled like a pile of shit writhing with bulging caterpillars and they are still swarming the bed, their speed growing with the expansion of their bodies. Her breath shortens and begins to come only in waves of screams as she flails off the bed and pushes as deep into the walls of her room as her body can press and she coils into a small child.

Can't you understand   she didn't have a *mother*.

The nurses in the ICU do not look us in the eye. They are quick and indifferent to our questions and quick and indifferent with my mother, as if to say there are people who deserve our help more, who deserve this bed more who didn't mean to die. Her catheter fills for hours and almost bursts onto the floor. Twelve hour shifts spent saving lives watching life snap like fire kindle and the sad, sad children and the sad, sad left-living and here a woman who tried.

Years & years. Can't you understand. A *mother*.

You are no more than four years old it is 1960something and a man with a pin on his lapel has come to your house to make your mother go away. He has come to save you from your mother he makes sure your daddy gets you forever your mother does not get to have you.

You are five years old and your mother calls the house and she says   I love getting fucked, he is fucking me so good right now. Railing me. I love to fuck. Your father is a terrible fuck he fucked around on me   you   hear? You hear me getting fucked?

You are five years old standing between your father and older sister. They have brought you to the mental institution to visit your mother and you are sobbing. A patient screams for gum, demands of you gum.

You are seven years old and the eye of the cast iron fireplace poker is making its way to your forehead. Your mother is going to   fucking kill you. Your brother's palm grabs her by the neck and you watch your mother's feet dangle above the ground. The poker strikes the fireplace and the wounded stone is left for decades.

You are ten, alone in the house and scared and peeing in the sink. Your father is in Poland for months your mother is gone or drunk or institutionalized. You are even younger, you are waking up to a house full of blood.

You are fourteen years old and realize you swallowed all the pills in the bathroom. You did   feel scared, very much so.

You are twenty-four and you marry your husband and inherit three children and grow your own baby in your belly. Your husband says he will not leave you & you are happy. You grow another baby in your belly.

You are mid thirties cleaning out the apartment of your dead mother. The scent of death still pungent poignant stagnant saccharine, the only smell that can saturate through the barriers of an old memory. You find: rings engraved with the Star of David, hoarded leather piled in bathtubs, jewelry stashed in the crevices of drawers, tables, walls, a picture of your oldest brother, condolences from neighbors who thought she had only one child. You say
there were four of us, four.

You are forty-two and your husband dies & leaves you & with five kids. You date too soon after & you try to stay sober & you drink again anyway & again & destroy & leave when you want & you did not want this.

You are fifty-one years old at a treatment center listening to a man with a pin on his lapel talk about recovery. You are walking up to him telling him about his pin and an outfit he was wearing forty something years ago and your father and your house in Highland Park. He says

yes, it was me. He says   how could you remember. He does not understand how you could remember.

You are fifty-two and it is Valentine's Day and there are still caterpillars on the window sill of the hospital room.

In pictures my grandmother looks like a spirit, or a haunting. Her eyes are dark, almost smirking, as if she knows a secret and it is divine and dark. She is strikingly beautiful. My mother says her hands were strong.

I tell my mom I want to know about Renée.

Renata   my mother says   if you try to find her, her name in Poland was Renata   I know nothing of Renata.

I ask   was she sick before?

My mother says   I think so   she must have been she was just   so dark.

      most likely raped most likely watched her mother murdered then her father murdered or taken to be murdered maybe siblings murdered before sent to work camp before a whole religion burrowed into her bones

A genetic inheritance, a chemical misfire, bones and bones of an unknowable ache.   Renata, Renata—

I try to find you. Your mother. Your story part
a part & apart from my story. I try to look for
you. I find only names. Your name is
[Renata] [Renée] [Renoe]

What is your name?

Mother, Greta. Father, Stanislaw. Born Lublin, Poland.
After these names I find only documents from after the
war. Naturalization. Marriage. Divorce. Address. Address.
Address.

I am looking for proof of your family's murder. I am
looking for proof of train ride to work camp. I am looking
for proof of boat ride to America. I am looking for proof
of religion. I am looking for proof of your god. I am
looking for proof of family. I am looking for proof of
mental illness. I am looking for proof of immigration. I am
looking I am looking for you I am looking for you I am
looking for you. What are you but a haunting. A terrible
mother. Renée dark eyes & a story Renoe a fresh
forgetting little Renata doe eyed child with bones in her
river.

I begin to hate you. I begin to think if I have a little girl I will name her after what you could have been. I begin to love you deeply. I stop looking. I begin to yearn for a knowing.

My oldest sister does not come to the hospital. She says
I hope you're okay, I hope she is okay. My brother
does not come to the hospital. His voicemail says
I'm sorry about her, I hope you're okay. Another sister
comes bedside at the hospital into a dying wake of
caterpillars and says   I'm not okay Mom I'm so sick of
this Mom I'm so mad at you Mom I don't want to see you
anymore   and then she stays for an hour and I do
not know why I dream of her inside out I dream of her a
purple bruise bleeding into the night until she is nothing
but needing until I can leave her sick and needing too.

It is me and my stepfather and the only sister still talking
to my mother until day four and my stepfather says
your mother kicked me out she's divorcing me from the
hospital bed he says to my sister   it's your fault
and your siblings are assholes and your stepmother is an
angel that wicked angel almost dying and divorcing and
they're so fucking mad and they're not fucking here
I love her   I love her.

My sister says to him   she is a tornado, and this time it
was you. I say to him   I told you she is a tornado, and
this time it was you. And I love you. And I'm sorry.

Blood and salt and caterpillar carcasses and last names everywhere.

۶۵

In a dream I have daughters.

Renata is a child when we leave for the hills and turn into another ridge. We travel at noon, empty and cold and without a place to move from. I carry her across my chest, I carry her firmly with both arms. We sing   they will hear us from a country away they will hear us hitting hard against our new territory. She asks   when   I tell her   we will leave when the ocean is right & ready to take back this tin cup stuffed full of star debris our debris.

My mother is a baby when we find the sea. I am already there. I embrace her across my chest, firmly with both arms. I emerge a sea urchin and I emerge a helpless thing drowning in air. Yellowing pockets of moon in my lungs. Almost too bright. I travel at noon, with a blue scarf and a tin cup for holding things.

۶۵

Google Search: Mauthausen Concentration Camp
Address: Erinnerungsstrabe 1, 4310 Mauthauseri, Austria
Hours: Closed Now

Google Search: Majdenek

    [. . . the walls were stained blue by Zykon B]

There are no survivors found under this name.

Renata

Renoe   *Banaszyck*   *unknown.*

Gutowski, Renee [ée]

age: 15 (+-) 5 years (?)

unknown.

Banashcheck   *Origin: Lublin*

unknown.   *Majdenek.*

Just one little girl appears in my mouth, suddenly crawling along my tongue. I spit her out onto my palm. She is damp and cross-legged. *You almost choked me* I tell her. *You didn't try very hard to look for me* she says. Her voice raises. *You didn't try very hard! You didn't try very hard!* I tap my collarbone with my thumbnail. *I didn't try very hard to look for you* I say. She calms. She hums while I write. She is gone before noon.

Origins attract beasts. When you weed a garden you pull from the roots and devour it whole.

≀●

Renata is a little girl with corn poppies weaved through
the ends of her thin black braids. Renata is a little girl who
rubs her toes on the edges of the Bystrzyca river, she likes
the slick moss & the wet solitude. Renata's first kiss is a
dare on the playground   no   Renata's first
word is mama   Renata's   no   Renata's
first dream is a straw the size of a bean stalk that sucks the
river dry and she runs with ready toes   wakes up
mama mama there were bones in the river   mama
mama my toes turned to poppies mama   I kissed
a boy last week on the playground and I want to marry
him mama mama   I love him what if the river is
sucked up to dry mama mama   what if a river—

≀●

As a child I jumped into the deep end of a pale blue pool. At the bottom I took a breath. I cannot remember the exhale, only the cool swelling of water, the relieved stretch of lung. Years later, I met a friend with the same story. In panic and laughter, we did not believe each other.

My sister says to my mother   I don't feel good with you in my life anymore I am taking me and your grandchild away from your life. I say   you goddamnit you we are trying to heal here you cruelthing we are trying to heal here mom is sober mom is trying mom is a better grandmother than mother mom is
my sister says   fine, heal. And I beg I say
          hey pleaseplease she is fragile we are trying to heal here. She says   fine, heal. I say   no no you do not understand her mother her mother our mother our orange wombs big stuff here. She says   why do you have to take this on? I say   look can you not see look look these little girls in my lap I am trying to dry them nearly dead in cold pond water just wait they are almost good as new—

                              ❧

          The little girl says she would like
          to jumprope now. I am out of
          toys, so I pluck a vein from my
          wrist and place the ends in her
          tiny hands. Go play
                              the adults are talking.

                              ❧

My sister is born so small & into the palm of my father's hand. Head & body, right in his grown palm. My sister is born so small & finally they can bring her home. At the end of the hospital hallway is my mother's mother & my mother says   what are you doing here   her spine cold with sweat & such terror & she says
do not touch the baby she is so small   & her mother wants to see the baby & my mother says   no do not touch her do not touch her she is too small.

My mother and father grow this baby next to my father's three babies who are children now & then my mother gives birth to me & my mother makes Valentine's baskets each year for us, such big bags with stomachs of candy and red tissue sticking out like an exclamation our hands ready & grabbing & filled & mom, mom!

My nephew is born & I spread my arms like lineage & I tell my sister   looklook   & I imagine she does not want to hold him & think of inheritance like how I hold me & think of inheritance & she does not want to ask questions & I do not want to ask the question of my sister & give answers like I cannot finish a truth without her like I do not want to give her anything & here she is with offering & here she is with offering & I do not want to share this tender excavation she swallows like oranges like train engines like babydoll heads like lemon burn like it tastes of her own daily spit while I plead look I plead look I plead notice I grow cold I hope for holding.

When my mother leaves the hospital I go into a depression it feels like waking up breathing grocery shopping waitressing driving fucking cooking depressed and I feel real silly because she lived and I feel real cold in the leftover winter.

& I am one hundred and twelve days and fifteen degrees below zero into this midwest winter and I am so sick of being cold and Hennepin Avenue is so sick of being cold. My lover all heat his heat so much softer than the radiator's. I am a cold half moon regurgitated into his elbows every hour.

& I am thirty minutes and some drinks into a naked sob on laminate kitchen tile, the world's most paltry lament on kitchen tile, unable to breathe about how I think there's a horror in the void and you have to either keep living or keep dying an endless tumble and you either have to keep living or keep dying and I think there's a circle and I'm tired and I don't even like a third drink or sobbing or a crying woman in the kitchen.

& I am a hundred dollar bill into an eightball my left atrium dropping through my ribcage my hand holding the cold thigh of a stripper she's nameless nipple like a planet in my mouth her nose in the corner of my credit card her lungs all inhale & blow little black eyed shasta daisy, little shaky pale bloom rising from my lap eyes wild little savage cloud I am hypothermic veins neon breath patterns I set

her on my lover's kneecaps he doesn't want her she leaves
into an eternity of laps he wants my eyes and I can no
longer tell the high from the comedown the cliché more
tragic than an overdose   I'm okayI'm okay
you're not supposed to stick the bill right into the bag
          I know justI'm okayI'm okay   take the
velvet rope to the sunrise would be so beautiful if
everything wasn't so electric plugged in heartbeat eclectic
coping   I'mokayI'm okay   I'll wake up
tomorrow for the sun and your collarbone and the cold
pizza in the fridge   I don't feel like a story tonight I
never feel like a story anymore.

& I am a half mile around Lake Calhoun and three hours
into a waitressing shift and four minutes past orgasm and
mid blue dream and mid sob exhale and after dope deal
and I am elbow in eye socket and I am womb in dahlia and
breath like gun fire all over and all over.

My   mama is my   c l o s e s tthing   is my closest

thing   my mother is my   mama is my closest   m o t

h e r   m y closest   thing   my   mother   is my

closest thing my mother is my thing closest   my mother

is   the   c l o s e s t   thing to me.

The psychiatrist says   statistically speaking
they will not attempt suicide twice   statistically
speaking my depression is normal/circumstantial/genetic/
in my head/a drowning sensation.

My earliest memory is a sour green glow in the left corner of a quivering darkness. It is nostalgic, itinerant, warm.

My skin brushed with mother. I cannot distinguish temperature. The meat of my small sole a tender push down. Breach baby. I develop a taste for salt. Too much sensation. Hyperglycemic baby such a bitter blood trying to sweeten.

With our luck   she'll float feet first in thirst for soil
her blood will damage the body   her stomach will
contract against its own milk   with our luck—

Renata, I have little to curate of you. Polish. French origin. Dark hair & green eyes. Sometimes, your face cracked open. A harem ring.

My mother finds a letter:

Renée; you hurt me very much by going over to the bootleggers in your panties & bra and staying 2 days. What can I say... I miss you very much, but something will work out for me. Good bye, good luck, and may your God bless you—

The frame starts around the bigness of a little girl. At the tips of her braids. *May your God*—Cuts 90 degrees at her hips. On the wood floor of a living room, a circle burn covered with rug. *May your God*—Bottom corner, a light switch. Bottom corner, lip to a birthwet forehead. Around me, or her, or her, *bless you*—

I have remade the frame from cedar I have burned the original I have chewed on its edges I have placed pictures over & over each other I have nailed them to walls, stomachs.

ॐ

In the spring my lover brings me to a lake and sets me in a boat. The water is both a cold womb and a deep graveyard. It is a wet lung for swelling gills, a bedroom of spines. There is something about the way my limbs feel during the birth of a morning. Loose, wild, very attached to body. There is a loon in my throat. A birchwood through my fingertips. He hooks a fish three casts in. The blue fishing net lays wet on the floor, eternally sturdy, hungry and open mouthed.

The fish is small but thick, meager fins but broad in the upper belly, he is a slow morphing of stretching bones, a little fish child playing make believe in a father's ribcage. We say we wish we had the energy to fillet him, to feel like wilderness again, to taste a fried lake in a buttered skillet, the conquer and re use. Remember that's earth all over your silverware. He takes the hook out and it sounds like wet tension, the pulling of a rain boot or a calloused foot on a porcelain bathtub. He sets the fish back into the water, holding its spine as it strikes firmly back and forth, delirium tremens shaking from the air. Ready to reenter the water through a wound. The press of palm and fingertip hold tightly to the meat of its back, a hearty farewell the fish does not hold onto. Suddenly it knows something greater and swims. I wonder if it remembers the world above, the inability to ever survive there.

she says   I am just happier without her in my life

she says   I never liked mermaids.

                  The thing about them

                  so trapped below.

I will blame you if she tries to kill herself again.
I write this on a piece of paper
chew it
for hours

swallow

please she's sick she's just sick.

When my mother gets sober she wakes up at 6 A.M. and deals with the dog she bought when she was drunk. She turns the volume high on a Red Hot Chili Peppers music video and she says she likes the part where Anthony Kiedis takes his shirt off. At night she makes chocolate malts with a man from treatment while my stepfather's Christmas decorations are piled into an idle lump in the basement. She says fuck when she is mad and she does not pretend to blush. She reads my father's love letters in the afternoon. He writes the moon is almost all whole. She makes an appointment for a blue morpho butterfly to be tattooed on her shoulder. She still cannot sit still. She is chasing death down a rabbit hole and laughing. We needy, stringy strands of souls keep gnawing at the ends of her. We buy neon signs and point them at our faces. We are desperate for her to catch glimpse of something to stay and watch a while.

I imagine her an exhausted circus manager, lips pink, bones dull. She stays late to let the little girl see the tiger before it's caged. She lets the smoke and mirrors suffocate her while the child sees the wonder of it all.

I muddle the picture of my grandmother in a blue dress into the picture of my mother in a blue dress into the picture of me in a blue dress make pretty soon make metaphor make meaning make mother out of us.

❧

The little girls say *There are at least a dozen more of us.*
They tug at my dress. *When you run out of bread which one*
will you feed which one of us will you feed will you save
which one of us which one gets to grow up?

❧

I ask my mother about her childhood. She says   I was
alone & so scared & peed in the sink.

& I repeated me as a child   & I repeated things
I hated all of this leaving   didn't realize   at the
time   you swear to god you   don't know any better
         I was dropped on this earth   out of
somewhere   and then   all I knew was
abandonment   would never leave   & so I—

I pay a man to tell me about myself. He says my womb and my mother's womb are indistinguishable. He says I should imagine my womb spinning clockwise, gentle and orange.

I buy an orange candle for my spinning orange lake, I sing into my orange lake, I write from the bottom of my orange lake, and from the surface, I piss into my orange lake, I slap its waters irreverently, I spin with such desperation its waters spill and I nearly drown just ankle deep, I bless my orange lake with nervous authority, I bleed for months.

My niece grows inside of my sister's belly & I say to my
sister   you have chosen our grandmother's
middle name for your little girl & my sister says   oh
& I plead with my sister   let her see them
& my sister says   no I am happy & I say   no
you are not !   which is a strange thing to argue & she
says   I am a mother that protects her children
          & I do not want to understand & I become a
child pleading & I become patronizing & cruel & then
tender & again desperate & I say   I can only beg of
you for this new little girl   & what I mean is these
three little girls are begging of you.

My mother says I was allergic to my own milk. Soy baby. I attached to my mother in other ways. For example, I tied the orange string to the end of her pinkie and I tied the other end to mine and ran towards the mountains.

❧

The three little girls sit crossed-legged at the end of my bed. *Go fish* says the littlest one, and the other two fidget with their skirts. *Ok* I say, *thank you.* They all close their eyes, tilt their heads back and open their mouths very wide. I cast my fishing line, which extends down the littlest one's throat and lands near the east end of her stomach. *Reel it in reel it in!* The other two sing. I reel in the line, and a bloodied acorn plops out the little girl's cheeks. She swallows the pooling blood in her mouth and clears her throat. The other two girls chew their mouths nervously. I clean the acorn off with my thumbs, and set it next to my knee. *Go fish* I offer, closing my eyes, tilting my head back, opening my mouth very wide.

❧

Renata, I didn't try very hard to look for you. I took letters, internet searches, a picture of you in a blue dress, a tongue trying to say your maiden name correctly, I sucked these right down the throat like a breath. Spat them back up a new thing. Something sweet to chew on, a salve, a story.

Renata, if you were better we would have craved your chubby fingers & forced rings over our knuckles & thought of you old & beautiful. The possibility of your hands terrify us. We do not want your history.

Renata, you thought of drowning in a river. You thought of stuffing your mouth with stone, a good way to choke. A good way to remove the throat. As inheritance, my mother is choking. As inheritance, there is a stone swelling in my mouth. I do not feel I can take a whole breath. My voice must pass over the hand of my mother, trying to dislodge stone from a locked trachea.

Renata, I cannot pronounce the river I gave you for your pretend girlhood. I fish a stone from the river with my mouth and inhale it into my throat. Choking now, I remember.

In the girlhood you gave my mother, you try and kill her with a cast iron fireplace poker. I gave you a red bow, I gave you hands.

Renata, in the end, my lover offers me your ring. It fits snug over my knuckles and rests delicately on my finger. I twirl it incessantly for weeks, until I can recognize it there. Did you know there is nothing to inherit?

R e n a t a did you say what you needed did you come through and throw sticks and find oranges under mattresses and tell me   spin clockwise and be clockwise   did you say what you needed to your two daughters your two sons their daughters and their sons did you mean it   are you excused   did you become what you needed did you come up pure little Katrine in your pond toes did you come up did you come up at all did you find what you needed did you find what you wanted to find in my body did you find what you needed to find in my body did you recognize a bone or a hand or the way in which I turned everyone into children all so strange and brown haired and almost resembling something of a ripening almost did you remember all whole to grab what you came for from under the wooden shelves your buttons a picture your child r e n a t a did you get what you came for a girlhood did you expect a girlhood from a child were you here for hers or hers or here are you excused there is more of you so many little girls what to do with them what to do.

If the body remembers everything she happened to me she
happened to me before I was something to be happened to
if the body remembers everything she happened—

say   other

say   and

❧

Three little girls
in three red dresses
to grandmother's house we go

the big bad wolf is in the forest
the big bad wolf is coming towards us
        to grandmother's house we go the wolf goes to
        grandmother's house we go the wolf goes to
        grandmother's house in grandmother's house

water rising up our throats
tails bursting from our coats

in grandmother's house the faces are mirrors for the others
our faces our mirrors
        so very much alike very much tin cups very much
        filled heads such lead dead very much such dead
        red red cups very much such brimful such very
        much alike very much alike girl would tell me no
        very much girl alike child hood very girl hood
        very alike child like very much such same very
        much alike

❧

Renata, 1978

Acknowledgements

Mom, I love you. Your support is unwavering and it holds me up each day.

"My mama is my closest thing" is a line I took from Ellie's grade school drawing to her mother. Bryan Sykes's book *The Seven Daughters of Eve* is where I learned about Katrine, and the seven mothers of the world. "The walls were stained with Zykon B" is a line from a History.com article "Holocaust Concentration Camps" that appeared from a Google search. A profound thank you to the United States Holocaust Memorial Museum for their database, resources, and dedication to Holocaust remembrance and the preservation of history.

Gratitude and love to Renata. To TJ & Niko—always, of course, & forever. To my family—WFIO—always. To Half Mystic Press, for caring about this story and giving it so much love. To Sara Veglahn and the entire Fall 2015 Memoir/Anti-Memoir workshop class at Naropa University. To Naropa University, the Jack Kerouac School of Disembodied Poetics, and Naropa University's Summer Writing Program. To Danielle Vogel, Shawnie Hamer, Gabrielle Lessans, Dani Ferrara, Jenni

Ashby, Jake Grieco, and Karolina Zapal, for their beautiful insights and support. To each and every one of my teachers I have encountered along the way, special thank you to David Welch and Barrie Jean Borich. To Minnesota, Chicago, and Colorado, who each gave pieces to this story.

About the Author

Marie Conlan is a Midwest poet living and writing in Colorado, where she is a co-collaborator with the .OFF collective and Nocturne Lucid Writing Workshops. She was named a finalist for the Noemi Press Book Award in 2017 and 2018, a finalist for the Airlie Press Prize in 2018, and a finalist for Metatron's 2018 Rising Authors Prize. She earned her MFA at the Jack Kerouac School of Disembodied Poetics at Naropa University. This is her first book.

CPSIA information can be obtained
at www.ICGtesting.com
Printed in the USA
BVHW051839140722
642166BV00004B/451

9 781948 552103